Gospel Bites

Cartoons by Joseph Noonan
Reflections by Joseph Nolan

Resource Publications, Inc.
San Jose, California

Editorial director: Kenneth Guentert
Managing editor: Elizabeth J. Asborno
Cover design & production: Huey Lee
Pasteup artist: Terri Ysseldyke-All

Reprint Department
Resource Publications, Inc.
160 E. Virginia Street #290
San Jose, CA 95112-5876

Library of Congress Cataloging in Publication Data
Noonan, Joseph, 1931-
    Gospel bites / cartoons by Joseph Noonan ;
    reflections by Joseph Nolan.
        p.   cm.
    ISBN 0-89390-239-X
    1. Bible. N.T. Gospels—Meditations. 2. Bible. N.T.
Gospels—Caricatures and cartoons. I. Nolan, Joseph. II. Title.
BS2555.4.N66 1992
263'.9—dc20   92-23076

96 95 94 93 92 | 5 4 3 2 1

The cartoons and reflections in this book were previously
published by Liturgical Publications Inc. (Sunday Publications)
in the "Good News" homily periodical.

Contents

Cycle A

Cycle B

Cycle C

Other Solemnities and Feasts of the Lord

CYCLE

A

FIRST SUNDAY OF ADVENT
Matthew 24:37-44

More and more,
Christmas becomes a lot of fuss.
From wearing out before
it happens,
Lord, deliver us!

SECOND SUNDAY OF ADVENT
Matthew 3:1-12

The fist, the stone, the gun
have shattered every age.
But is it possible to turn a page
and begin a history, not of war but peace,
when brother killing brother finally will cease?

THIRD SUNDAY OF ADVENT
Matthew 11:2-11

You heard of John the Baptizer
but what did you go out to see?
A man who bends, like marsh grass,
or stands tall, like a mighty tree?
You looked for a prophet, and found him.
Now discover the kingdom of God.

FOURTH SUNDAY OF ADVENT
Matthew 1:18-24

Blest are those who listen
and give welcome to the word!
My flesh as well as spirit
magnifies the Lord.

CHRISTMAS (December 25)

God's poverty—a sure disguise
to keep him hid from human eyes.
We don't seem to understand
that he favors the poor of the land!

HOLY FAMILY
Matthew 2:13-15, 19-23

Who is this child, and why this flight,
this desperate journey in the night?
He is Moses, Israel, all in one,
and out of Egypt he will come
to set us free, to teach a new commandment.

MARY, MOTHER OF GOD (January 1)
Luke 2:16-21

Angels depart and shepherds return,
Magi go home by another way.
A carpenter and his wife are left
To keep the secret of God's love.

EPIPHANY
Matthew 2:1-12

There's room in Juda for only one crown!
Herod is right to be upset,
to ponder a message he can't forget:
a king born in Bethlehem town.

BAPTISM OF THE LORD
Matthew 3:13-17

The devil, you say!
Well, something's in the way
of doing, when we hear it,
the voice of the Spirit.

FIRST SUNDAY IN LENT
Matthew 4:1-11

Our piety is practical.
We give money when it's tax deductible.
We fast to make up for our gluttony
and pray devoutly almost every Sunday.
So who needs Lent? (We do!)

SECOND SUNDAY IN LENT
Matthew 17:1-9

The carpenter from Nazareth
who calls us his friends,
can this be the one
the Father sends?
Jesus! What do we do now?

LOOK, MARY, DOESN'T YOUR SON KNOW THAT THOSE SAMARITAN FRIENDS OF HIS ARE SOCIALLY INFERIOR TYPES WHO RUIN EVERY NEIGHBORHOOD THEY MOVE INTO?

THIRD SUNDAY IN LENT
John 4:5-42

Jesus' guest list is not very selective:
Sinners. Women. Pagans.
Tax collectors. Samaritans.
And even us.

FOURTH SUNDAY IN LENT
John 9:1-41

"Do you have hospitalization,
or an appointment today?"
It's easier to get to Jesus!
Office hours night and day.

FIFTH SUNDAY IN LENT
John 11:1-45

Back to life, to war and taxes.
And yes, you're right—to tribulation.
We'll take it. But really, Jesus,
we'd prefer a new creation!

PASSION/PALM SUNDAY
Matthew 26:14-27, 66

Follow him! (But not too close.)
Yell hosannah (words are cheap).
Crowds melt away.
And night returns.

16

EASTER
John 20:1-9

Last at the cross, first at the tomb,
first to see the risen Lord—
the disciples do not take their word.
"This is women's talk!" they say.
(It's a bias still around today.)

SECOND SUNDAY OF EASTER
John 20:19-31

Thomas, do not doubt or grieve.
We live, we die, we need a friend.
What we discover is God's love for us.
That's all that's needed in the end.

THIRD SUNDAY OF EASTER
Luke 24:13-35

We'll stop at the inn,
have a drink and a bite.
Tell the stranger to join us;
it's getting towards night.
I wonder who he is.

FOURTH SUNDAY OF EASTER
John 10:1-10

If you had your wish
would you rather be called
a sheep or a fish?
Don't take it hard! It's only a sample
of what the gospel uses for an example!

FIFTH SUNDAY OF EASTER
John 14:1-12

What's really real? Does Jesus rise
only to hide from human eyes?
Is God a Father or a force,
primeval egg, creation's source?
We'll have to wait and just find out
what this believing's all about.

SIXTH SUNDAY OF EASTER
John 15:9-17

We'd like our religion
to be comforting and gentle.
It is. But the love Jesus teaches
is not sentimental.

SEVENTH SUNDAY OF EASTER
John 17:1-11

Is it really ending,
the days he walked the earth?
Is something called church coming to birth?
Yes. It's Jesus
re-entering our life.

23

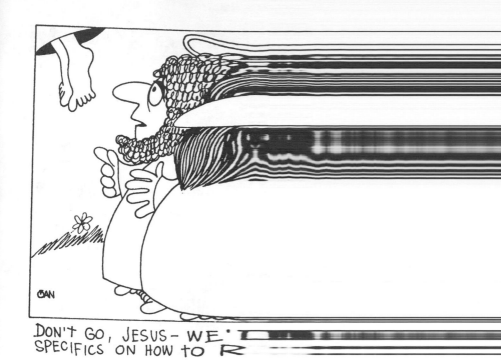

DON'T GO, JESUS - WE ...
SPECIFICS ON HOW TO R

ASCENSION
Matthew 28:16-20

To run a church or to live a lif...
   the question? To be an org...
   or a spirit-filled and love-ch...
   Perhaps it is the best of bot...
The Body of Christ comes aliv...
   Christ. The word takes flesh...
   And we discover that he's s...

PENTECOST
John 20:19-23

What God wishes—
things that ought to be—
the Holy Spirit pushes.
But there's no monopoly!
We have to listen—to each other.

25

HOLY TRINITY
John 3:16-18

"In the name of the Father,
Son, and Spirit."
That's the best we can do, God!
Have we come very near it?

CORPUS CHRISTI
John 6:51-58

Eucharist means thanksgiving—
thanks for the body of Christ
which we are, which we become.
No wonder we fumble for words
to explain so great a gift.
Bread. Body. Us. Christ.

THE LORD WAS BAPTIZED IN THIS RIVER,
SO I THINK WE'RE SWIMMING IN HOLY
WATER.

SECOND SUNDAY OF THE YEAR
John 1:29-34

Not even Niagara Falls
can wash away sin.
But baptism is a sign.
Water flows over me
and so does God's love.

THIRD SUNDAY OF THE YEAR
Matthew 4:12-23

So long ago he preached the word,
sent out the call,
healed the sick, and died upon the cross.
In a computer "cost analysis"
would all this come up loss?
We could answer beginning with ourselves.

FOURTH SUNDAY OF THE YEAR
Matthew 5:1-12

Are there no gospel words to bless
the rich as well as poor?
Yes. But the poor and lowly
have the inside track, for sure!

FIFTH SUNDAY OF THE YEAR
Matthew 5:13-16

Parishioner's prayer:
Lord, make me pious
and full of good cheer,
but don't expect me
to volunteer!

31

SIXTH SUNDAY OF THE YEAR
Matthew 5:17-37

The leer, the sneer,
the murder in the heart—
in these Jesus' followers
can have no part.

SEVENTH SUNDAY OF THE YEAR
Matthew 5:38-48

I pray, give tithes,
and practice clean living.
I'm just not keen
on all this forgiving.
(Jesus—is this commandment necessary?)

EIGHTH SUNDAY OF THE YEAR
Matthew 6:24-34

The Teacher is not telling us
to cease providing for another day.
Rather, he is reminding us
that all we really know about tomorrow
is that God is part of it. So relax.

IN CHURCH I LEARNED ABOUT BUILDING ON ROCK, NOT SAND.

NINTH SUNDAY OF THE YEAR
Matthew 7:21-27

Death is the tide.
It surges in upon the shore
and all our castles are no more.
Death is the tide. But Christ is the rock,
and we endure.

© 1992 Resource Publications, Inc. 35

TENTH SUNDAY OF THE YEAR
Matthew 9:9-13

Go tell the sun,
"Shine only on the good!"
You'll have as much luck telling God
to love only the best of us.

ELEVENTH SUNDAY OF THE YEAR
Matthew 9:36 - 10:8

Twelve men get the call.
We mustn't think that's all!
There's no discrimination
in the new creation.
God is an equal opportunity employer.

TWELFTH SUNDAY OF THE YEAR
Matthew 10:26-33

The word of God is often misread!
The word is really Jesus in the flesh
and those who live by his Spirit
setting us free by their love.

THIRTEENTH SUNDAY OF THE YEAR
Matthew 10:37-42

Jesus didn't say,
"Take up my aluminum cross."
He calls us to the unknown.
And our only hope is that he is with us.

FOURTEENTH SUNDAY OF THE YEAR
Matthew 11:25-30

The Savior rode an ass,
the scripture says.
It must have taken quite a while.
But the chariot, the warrior's horse,
(Mercedes, too?)
just didn't fit his style.

FIFTEENTH SUNDAY OF THE YEAR
Matthew 13:1-23

One time the prophet said for God,
"My word is a hammer to break rocks."
Could it break through my defenses, Lord?
My super-ego, made of concrete?
The word of the Lord. Watch out.

SIXTEENTH SUNDAY OF THE YEAR
Matthew 13:24-43

Theologians like to speak of mystery
and say that's why there's parable and poetry.
But also preaching—to make the point more
  clear.
And praying—to bring the Spirit near.

SEVENTEENTH SUNDAY OF THE YEAR
Matthew 13:44-52

Attention, yes. Comprehension, no.
Parable teaching is rather slow!
Oh, sure we understand, they say.
Don't you believe it.

EIGHTEENTH SUNDAY OF THE YEAR
Matthew 14:13-21

Today it is bread and wine
that is the sign
by which he feeds the multitude.
It is no ordinary food
but bread of life, and cup of joy.

NINETEENTH SUNDAY OF THE YEAR
Matthew 14:22-33

A baby's first step
and a dying man's last need
is for the word of love
that says, "Come! I am here
when you fall."

TWENTIETH SUNDAY OF THE YEAR
Matthew 15:21-28

A woman and a foreigner—two strikes
even before the disciples say, "Get rid of her!"
But love endures all things. It perseveres.
And wins the victory. The teacher hears
her plea—and heals her child.

LET ME GUESS — YOU'RE A LITTLE CONCERNED ABOUT BEING TOO WOBBLY A ROCK FOR JESUS' CHURCH TO STAND ON . . . .

TWENTY-FIRST SUNDAY OF THE YEAR
Matthew 16:13-20

We build the church every day
without applause or bands playing
if we believe, like Peter,
and our lives are the clue to others
that Christ is still on earth.

TWENTY-SECOND SUNDAY OF THE YEAR
Matthew 16:21-27

We're strong on comfort, Lord.
Haven't you got
a kind of disciple who's not
eager to be a martyr or saint?
Those great ambitions make me faint.

I FIND BRETHREN EASIER TO LOVE IN THE ABSTRACT—
UP CLOSE THEY'RE ALL PEOPLE WITH
PROBLEMS....

TWENTY-THIRD SUNDAY OF THE YEAR
Matthew 18:15-20

The only trouble is—
The God who is love didn't stay in the abstract!
He could have been such a comfortable,
    philosophical God—easy to worship.
Instead he got involved with people. People
    with problems.

TWENTY-FOURTH SUNDAY OF THE YEAR
Matthew 18:21-35

I can't forgive, much less forget.
I like the taste, the thought, of getting even.
Jesus' words are not for me.
But—I would also like to enter heaven!

TWENTY-FIFTH SUNDAY OF THE YEAR
Matthew 20:1-16

The gospel (or God's love) has funny ideas
   about success.
If you come in second (or not at all)—
when they choose up a team,
you can still be first with this Jesus.

TWENTY-SIXTH SUNDAY OF THE YEAR
Matthew 21:28-32

The church is "the gathered community."
Only some are scattered!
Those modest folk who think
their presence never mattered.
It does, though. The body of
   Christ—remember?
Don't make it short a member.

TWENTY-SEVENTH SUNDAY OF THE YEAR
Matthew 21:33-43

God works with broken sticks,
reclaims our wasted days.
(There must be other ways, you scream.)
There are. But if you fail the first time,
you still can make the team.

TWENTY-EIGHTH SUNDAY OF THE YEAR
Matthew 22:1-14

Jesus, will you explain
your latest parable, please?
No answer. Our only hope
is to hear those homilies!

TWENTY-NINTH SUNDAY OF THE YEAR
Matthew 22:15-21

But did he ever tell us
what we should give to God?
Yes. You shall love the Lord your God
with all your strength.
With all your heart and mind.
He is the One. There is no other.

THIRTIETH SUNDAY OF THE YEAR
Matthew 22:34-40

It is the presence of God in another
that makes such a one
my sister or brother.
All the world is kin.
We are connected. We are family—
and divided only by our sin.

THIRTY-FIRST SUNDAY OF THE YEAR
Matthew 23:1-12

Humility is all futility,
or so most people say.
But don't be too sure.
God's promises are all
for the humble and the poor.

THIRTY-SECOND SUNDAY OF THE YEAR
Matthew 25:1-13

Mark and Matthew, John and Luke—
is it plan or just a fluke
no woman wrote a gospel?
Men as always lead the way
(except at the cross, and on Easter Day.)

THIRTY-THIRD SUNDAY OF THE YEAR
Matthew 25:14-30

"Industrious and reliable servants
needed for Jesus to employ."
Pay is poor. But at the end, a bonus:
"Come, share your Master's joy."

CHRIST THE KING
Matthew 25:31-46

The mansions of the rich
and the titles of the great—
all these will pass away.
But the Lordship of Jesus, his grace and power
is here to stay.

CYCLE

B

FIRST SUNDAY OF ADVENT
Mark 13:33-37

The gospel does sound wild!
Where is gentle Jesus, meek and mild?
He's still around. Just don't miss
the time of his visitation.

A DIET OF WILD HONEY AND LOCUSTS IS ENOUGH TO MAKE ANYBODY CRY IN THE WILDERNESS!

SECOND SUNDAY OF ADVENT
Mark 1:1-8

John also wore a camel's hair coat
and a leather belt
(which doesn't sound too bad).
He also shouted, "Get ready!
God is preparing his big surprise!"

THIRD SUNDAY OF ADVENT
John 1:6-8, 19-28

There is a darkness
that covers up our deeds
and others' needs.
A darkness of the heart.
Not knowing. Not caring.

FOURTH SUNDAY OF ADVENT
Luke 1:26-38

Who builds a house for the Lord?
David.
But it had to wait a thousand years
and for a young girl to say yes.

CHRISTMAS (December 25)

Jingle, jingle all the way
to the bank—What did you say?
"Remember, Christ your Savior
was born on Christmas day."

HOLY FAMILY
Luke 2:22-40

When he's grown up
they will be asking,
"Can anything good come out of Nazareth?"
God says: "My ways are not your ways."

MARY, MOTHER OF GOD (January 1)
Luke 2:16-21

We lose you, Jesus,
lose you for sure
if your accommodations
are among the very poor.

EPIPHANY
Matthew 2:1-12

And sometimes our minds ache
with truths too deep,
our hearts ache
when we think we are unloved.
Then, like the kings, we need to find him
and discover it's alright.

BAPTISM OF THE LORD
Mark 1:7-11

Let it be, let it be,
for Jesus became one of us.
Like us, he prays. Suffers. Dies.
Like him, we try to love. And live.

FIRST SUNDAY IN LENT
Mark 1:12-15

Fast, give alms, and pray—
isn't there some other way?
Yes. Try serenity for Lent.
Fast from grumbling and complaining.
Try patience for a day!

SECOND SUNDAY IN LENT
Mark 9:2-10

With burdens bent we plod
our ordinary ways
and suddenly God
illumines our days
with a light that is more
than anything we have known before.

THIRD SUNDAY IN LENT
John 2:13-25

We don't want our customary lives
to get out of joint,
and so, with Lent and gospels
we often miss the point!

FOURTH SUNDAY IN LENT
John 3:14-21

More precious than silver and gold,
from no ordinary mold
God made me. There can only be
one thing greater to say:
He loves me.

FIFTH SUNDAY IN LENT
John 12:20-33

To die and rise
should happen every day
but not everybody buys
such a drastic way
to come alive.

BUT HE'S WORTH MORE THAN 30 PIECES OF SILVER!

PASSION/PALM SUNDAY
Mark 14:1-15, 47

Love has no price.
A million would not suffice.
Judas measures his worth by greed.
The rest of us by our need.

B

EASTER
John 20:1-9

We have not invented the words
to explain the resurrection.
It is the last, great deed of love.
The heart alone understands.

SECOND SUNDAY OF EASTER
John 20:19-31

Thomas was a sensible man.
And crucifixion wasn't in the plan.
Nor resurrection. What's a man to do
with women's wild reports? And visions, too?
Believe, Thomas. Strange things are true.

THIRD SUNDAY OF EASTER
Luke 24:35-48

Who can count God's surprises?
He even surprised us by being born.
And by dying.
But the one called resurrection
is the best surprise of all.

79

FOURTH SUNDAY OF EASTER
John 10:11-18

They left their nets and boats and kin
when he said, "Come, and follow me."
What was the secret of his appeal?
Easy. He loved them.

FIFTH SUNDAY OF EASTER
John 15:1-8

We tend to droop into easy chairs
and nod off during sermons.
We are not all high achievers.
And still you love us. A patient lover, Lord.

SIXTH SUNDAY OF EASTER
John 15:9-17

Religion's not easy to define.
For some, authority is big.
Keep the commandments, toe the line!
For others, feeling is the thing.
Life is wonderful, everything is fine.
(Something more needs to be said!)

SEVENTH SUNDAY OF EASTER
John 17:11-19

Yes, Jesus, you left too much of the world
still unredeemed
and too many things for us to do.
Shake us awake. We might come to realize
that we aren't doing them by ourselves.

ASCENSION

You chose us, Lord. You must recall
we never claimed to know it all.
We don't even have a degree
in counseling or prophecy.
(Come, Holy Spirit!)

PENTECOST
John 20:19-23

Pilgrim, still your fears.
For a thousand years
are but a day in his sight,
a watch in the night.
(It is still God's world.)

HOLY TRINITY
Matthew 28:16-20

God is a circle, never a square.
God is a point that's everywhere.
God is one but God is three.
And God, I admit, is a mystery!

CORPUS CHRISTI
Mark 14:12-16, 22-26

Don't worry if you get it wrong.
The secret is, that you belong!
"The body of Christ." Speak up. Remember,
Baptism makes you a charter member.

SECOND SUNDAY OF THE YEAR
John 1:35-42

The fish stories will be told to us—
of crowds that hunger and are fed,
of nets that swell with sudden catch.
They are Jesus-stories.
Tales of power and love.

THIRD SUNDAY OF THE YEAR
Mark 1:14-20

Jesus came to end those deeds
that lead to prejudice and fraction.
In the kingdom of God you'll see
there's no need for affirmative action!

FOURTH SUNDAY OF THE YEAR
Mark 1:21-28

"I confess to almighty God
and to you, my brothers and sisters."
It's true that we don't shout,
But evil spirits still go out.

FIFTH SUNDAY OF THE YEAR
Mark 1:29-39

There's plenty of ailments left.
The miracles seem fewer today.
Or is the miracle of healing
what the physician and the friend
are doing all the time?

91

SIXTH SUNDAY OF THE YEAR
Mark 1:40-45

What has God done for you today?
There's no longer any problem
with giving thanks or shouting hurrah.
The problem now is us.
We take his gifts for granted.

SEVENTH SUNDAY OF THE YEAR
Mark 2:1-12

It's really a lot easier
to get your sins forgiven!
But it's great to have friends
who want to share the best with you.
Like the gospel. Like Jesus Christ.

ABOUT JESUS' GREAT PARABLE ON WINE AND
WINE.SKINS— WELL, WE'VE GOT TWELVE
DIFFERENT INTERPRETATIONS GOING HERE.

EIGHTH SUNDAY OF THE YEAR
Mark 2:18-22

Don't worry if you're not a scripture scholar.
The apostles weren't. And they got the word.
The secret is called the Holy Spirit
who helps both the learned and the simple
to stand in the presence. To hear the Good
   News.

NINTH SUNDAY OF THE YEAR
Mark 2:23 - 3:6

The best we can do on the Sabbath
is the Eucharist: The word of God,
the body and blood of Christ,
the communion of heaven and earth.
Is that miracle enough?

TENTH SUNDAY OF THE YEAR
Mark 3:20-35

The speech is blunt but Mary knows
the truth of what the Rabbi says.
The one who does the Father's will
belongs to the family of God.

ELEVENTH SUNDAY OF THE YEAR
Mark 4:26-34

We planted the seed
and perhaps we forgot
that it's God who gives the increase.
Are we "too busy about many things?"

TWELFTH SUNDAY OF THE YEAR
Mark 4:35-41

The tides of death roll over us
and why does Jesus sleep?
But he asks another question:
"Why are you fearful,
O you of little faith?"

THIRTEENTH SUNDAY OF THE YEAR
Mark 5:21-43

Jesus raised the dead to life
with a touch. A word. And faith.
We might revive a friendship (or a parish)
if we met. And talked. And prayed.

FOURTEENTH SUNDAY OF THE YEAR
Mark 6:1-6

Don't let a little failure
or discouragement get you down.
There's no profit being a prophet
with the gang in the old hometown!

FIFTEENTH SUNDAY OF THE YEAR
Mark 6:7-13

There's no insurance policy
that saves from death
or guarantees forgiveness...
But isn't that what we mean
by Jesus? And his Father?

SIXTEENTH SUNDAY OF THE YEAR
Mark 6:30-34

The Good Shepherd's part's OK.
But if we could get our wish
we'd like a new image
instead of sheep and fish!

SEVENTEENTH SUNDAY OF THE YEAR
John 6:1-15

Keep the sermon exegetical—
tell us how it happened long ago.
A preacher shouldn't be political
or disturb us in our status quo.

EIGHTEENTH SUNDAY OF THE YEAR
John 6:24-35

Is there a formula
for those who wish to live?
Yes. Love as he loves,
forgive as he forgives.

NINETEENTH SUNDAY OF THE YEAR
John 6:41-51

I learned of God, the scholar said.
I studied night and day.
I love my neighbor, said another.
It was a quicker way!

TWENTIETH SUNDAY OF THE YEAR
John 6:51-58

Ours not to question why.
Ours but to follow.
But Jesus! Could you sugar-coat
the words we have to swallow?

TWENTY-FIRST SUNDAY OF THE YEAR
John 6:60-69

He throws us for a loss
with "Eat my body. Take your cross."
I think the Master's saying
discipleship is more than praying!

TWENTY-SECOND SUNDAY OF THE YEAR
Mark 7:1-8, 14-15, 21-23

We know our way is better
and you be sure you hear it!
We run things by the letter.
Don't confuse us with the spirit!

TWENTY-THIRD SUNDAY OF THE YEAR
Mark 7:31-37

You'll hear something called Good News:
that God is your Father.
Your sins are forgiven.
God is love. Life is worth it.
Go tell the whole world.

LOOK, TO SELL CHRISTIANITY, YOU STRESS "FOLLOW ME" AND GO LIGHT ON "TAKE UP THE CROSS".

TWENTY-FOURTH SUNDAY OF THE YEAR
Mark 8:27-35

The gentle Jesus meek and mild
is always easier to take.
But the one we follow is the Crucified One.
Easter doesn't come cheaply.

TWENTY-FIFTH SUNDAY OF THE YEAR
Mark 9:30-37

If you put on the mind of a child,
laugh easily, make everyone your friend,
be full of wonder, love for life,
you will find the kingdom in the end.

TWENTY-SIXTH SUNDAY OF THE YEAR
Mark 9:38-43, 45, 47-48

A literal interpretation
is what it's all about!
But if your eye offend you,
do you go and pluck it out?
(Something more is needed!)

TWENTY-SEVENTH SUNDAY OF THE YEAR
Mark 10:2-16

Of wedded love, God said
For this cause, leave
father and mother,
and to each other cleave.

TWENTY-EIGHTH SUNDAY OF THE YEAR
Mark 10:17-30

If you want treasure for sure,
sell what you have, and give to the poor.
The treasure isn't all in heaven.
Some earthly rewards are also given.

TWENTY-NINTH SUNDAY OF THE YEAR
Mark 10:35-45

This Jesus doesn't swerve
from insisting that we serve!
And if they want to be holy
the proud had better be lowly.

THIRTIETH SUNDAY OF THE YEAR
Mark 10:46-52

I don't know where he studied
or got his degrees
all I know
is that he heard my pleas.

THIRTY-FIRST SUNDAY OF THE YEAR
Mark 12:28-34

We'd like to hate a little
(at least on some days).
But God reminds us:
"My ways are not your ways."

THIRTY-SECOND SUNDAY OF THE YEAR
Mark 12:38-44

Some find it hard
with money to part.
Some open purses
and some their heart.

THIRTY-THIRD SUNDAY OF THE YEAR
Mark 13:24-32

Apocalypse now or later?
God knows but isn't telling.
But there is good news in the land—the
kingdom of God is at hand!

CHRIST THE KING
John 18:33-37

Nations quake and kingdoms end;
trumpets hail the Lord of glory.
Children tell a different story.
"This is Jesus. Meet my friend."

CYCLE

C

FIRST SUNDAY OF ADVENT
Luke 21:25-28, 34-36

"The Lord increase you, make you overflow
with love for others as you go!"
Thus Paul encourages us
when life discourages us.

SECOND SUNDAY OF ADVENT
Luke 3:1-6

You really should take the whole thing in!
It's more than turning away from sin.
It's a herald declaring
a new day will begin.

THIRD SUNDAY OF ADVENT
Luke 3:10-18

Blue chips may falter
and investments not come true.
But Jesus comes for stockbrokers!
(And window washers, too.)

FOURTH SUNDAY OF ADVENT
Luke 1:39-45

Buy the wreaths and get some holly;
mail the cards; we've got to hurry;
shop and rush and charge and worry—
who said, "'Tis the season to be jolly!"

CHRISTMAS (December 25)

To shepherds and their sheep
and oxen in a stall,
to a carpenter and his wife,
to folk both great and small
he comes—the babe of Bethlehem
whose love will save us all.

HOLY FAMILY
Luke 2:41-52

A child sits in the temple.
He is the temple's Lord.
He listens to the learned men.
He is the incarnate Word.
He is also one of us, the human race.
And grows in wisdom, age, and grace.

YES, HE DOES LOOK AS IF
HE'D MAKE A GOOD SHEPHERD.

MARY, MOTHER OF GOD (January 1)
Luke 2: 16-21

There is a mystery
about this child that even we,
who call him son, must see.
What will this one grow up to be?

EPIPHANY
Matthew 2:1-12

Well might Herod fear
to lose a crown.
This king has power to turn
the whole world upside-down!

BAPTISM OF THE LORD
Luke 3:15-16, 21-22

If we really knew the glory
of Jesus as divine,
the stars would tremble
and the sun refuse to shine.
Humanity reveals him
and also conceals him.

DON'T ASK ME WHAT KIND OF TEMPTATIONS YOU
CAN HAVE ON A DESERT — ASK JESUS!

FIRST SUNDAY IN LENT
Luke 4:1-13

The devil can sit at the family table
or at the Board of Directors' meeting.
Evil is ubiquitous—everywhere.
So is goodness. That's why we have hope.

LORD, SCRIPTURE SCHOLARS ARE BOUND TO ASK IF THIS TRANSFIGURATION IS TO BE TAKEN LITERALLY OR FIGURATIVELY.

SECOND SUNDAY IN LENT
Luke 9:28-36

Scholars still plod their way
to find what happened on that day.
Was the light on Tabor rising sun
that fell upon the Risen One?
Come, let us adore him.

THIRD SUNDAY IN LENT
Luke 13:1-9

But with the help of the Spirit
we'll give a pretty good guess!
He wasn't a farmer looking for figs.
He was the divine lover, looking for love.
We are the fig tree. Fruitless still?

FOURTH SUNDAY IN LENT
Luke 15:1-3, 11-32

It's always easier to admire than imitate
the generosity of God,
easier to be on the receiving end
of forgiveness and love.
Let's not evade the issue. God is looking for
givers!

FIFTH SUNDAY IN LENT
John 8:1-11

Clean out sin, stamp out sinners! Oh yes?
You'll discover nobody's left.
We listen to this discomforting rabbi
as the stones fall from our hands.

PASSION/PALM SUNDAY
Luke 22:14-23, 56

The Last Supper was "men only."
But at the cross, except for John,
and at the tomb on Easter morn
you'll find it's "women only!"

EASTER
Luke 24:1-12

Their excited story fails;
the apostles call it women's tales!
But their testimony is true.
(The resurrection becomes more convincing
when the Lord is risen in you!)

SECOND SUNDAY OF EASTER
John 20:19-31

Who's dead now?
Who's mired in doubt and confusion?
It's Thomas and his friends
who need a resurrection!
Come, unlock the doors of the heart.

THIRD SUNDAY OF EASTER
John 21:1-19

Peter, if Christians have a wish,
it's not to be poor fish!
Don't bait us, hook us, haul us in.
Love us. Brothers, sisters. Let's begin!

FOURTH SUNDAY OF EASTER
John 10:27-30

There's reason to sing!
To laugh, break bread, enjoy everything.
Christ is risen, Lord on high,
no more to hurt, no more to die.
He is the Way.
And every dawn is Easter Day.

FIFTH SUNDAY OF EASTER
John 13:31-33, 34-35

A wise man named Chesterton
got the priorities straight.
He said, "Things must be loved first
and improved afterwards."

SIXTH SUNDAY OF EASTER
John 14:23-29

Jesus left a Church to teach us
and a ministry to preach us
the good news of our salvation.
(He also had to leave the Paraclete
to save us from total confusion!)

SEVENTH SUNDAY OF EASTER
John 17:20-26

There's no doubt our feelings have been
  slanted
to look out for Number One.
But the Lord takes for granted
a new commandment has begun.

ASCENSION
Luke 24:46-53

Before your Big Departure, Lord,
would you record a message, let us know
the right decisions, ways to go?
Relax. You still can get the word.
The messenger—if you can hear it—
is called the Holy Spirit.

PENTECOST
John 20:19-23

My Father's love is like the sea
and all my sins are cast therein,
like stones a boy throws from the shore.
They disappear. They are no more.

HOLY TRINITY
John 16:12-15

The whole truth and nothing but the truth
is that God is love, and loves you.
Sinners, rock fans, senior citizens,
tax collectors. Women, too.

CORPUS CHRISTI
Luke 9:11-17

The brain will always boggle here.
God is seeking more the will.
"Amen" is "yes." I do believe
the Lord, the Lord is with us still!

SECOND SUNDAY OF THE YEAR
John 2:1-12

There's no doubt
that Jesus works fast!
The steward's right. He saved
the best wine till the last.

THIRD SUNDAY OF THE YEAR
Luke 1:1-4; 4:14-21

He learned his letters in this place!
Now, suddenly
he no longer reads the prophecy
but declares it fulfilled.
The word goes out to every land:
the kingdom is at hand.

FOURTH SUNDAY OF THE YEAR
Luke 4:21-30

Throw the prophets out (or kill them).
Their words just make us nervous.
And then let's all get back
to a good religious service!

HAVE MIXED EMOTIONS, LORD, ABOUT A MIRACLE THAT SINKS MY BOAT.

FIFTH SUNDAY OF THE YEAR
Luke 5:1-11

The Lord has a way of being generous.
One loaf becomes five thousand.
Wine runs over; fish fight to get on the hook.
He even makes a promise about life.
He says it will be everlasting.

C

I TRY TO BECOME JERUSALEM'S YOUNG BUSINESSMA
OF THE YEAR; THEN I HEAR, "WOE TO YOU WHEN AL
SPEAK WELL OF YOU."

SIXTH SUNDAY OF THE YEAR
Luke 6:17, 20-26

It's hard to please this Jesus.
We don't want to be poor, or hungry, or
    failures.
But if we are, in spite of ourselves,
he's telling us we still belong.

SEVENTH SUNDAY OF THE YEAR
Luke 6:27-38

Jesus gives a lot of impractical advice
like: love your enemies, and lend without
    interest.
Our practical world has so many troubles
maybe we should give him a second hearing.

EIGHTH SUNDAY OF THE YEAR
Luke 6:39-45

Some of us have perfect vision
for seeing defects in other people.
Specks in their character, so to speak.
We just can't see
the planks in our own.

NINTH SUNDAY OF THE YEAR
Luke 7:1-10

What strange things are here!
Jews who tell of a Roman's goodness.
A master concerned for his servant.
An outsider who believes in Jesus.
Wonders all.

TENTH SUNDAY OF THE YEAR
Luke 7:11-17

He returns to a life
of taxes, worries, war and strife.
(Same old thing.)
The bigger plan is resurrection—
nothing less than a new creation.

ELEVENTH SUNDAY OF THE YEAR
Luke 7:36 - 8:3

No, she dried them with her hair!
She washed them with her tears,
this woman "known to be a sinner."
Her single deed of love
has been told through all the years.

TWELFTH SUNDAY OF THE YEAR
Luke 9:18-24

The savior's words (at times)
can throw us for a loss.
"Each day," he said, "take up my cross.
There are no days off. And follow in my steps."

THIRTEENTH SUNDAY OF THE YEAR
Luke 9:51-62

The disciples asked him
what to expect, what would be theirs.
He said, "Birds have nests
and foxes, lairs.
You and I will have the open sky.
And my Father's work—while there is time."

FOURTEENTH SUNDAY OF THE YEAR
Luke 10:1-12, 17-20

To love my neighbor, pray and sing
and all that stuff is fine!
But it wouldn't be funny
if we began to lose money
from following the gospel line.

FIFTEENTH SUNDAY OF THE YEAR
Luke 10:25-37

Sure I'll help (when I'm not busy).
Lend a hand, but later on.
Love my neighbor? Yes, provided
I can wait until he's gone.

SIXTEENTH SUNDAY OF THE YEAR
Luke 10:38-42

But Mary is not talking.
She is listening. Hearing the word.
If we weren't so busy
we, too, might have heard
that your word, O Lord, is life.

SEVENTEENTH SUNDAY OF THE YEAR
Luke 11:1-13

Dear God, here's my shopping list.
And please don't tell me you know best
what's good for me.
None of your mixed blessings now!

EIGHTEENTH SUNDAY OF THE YEAR
Luke 12:13-21

Of Jesus' warning, who takes heed?
Build bigger barns—and bigger cars!
Who cares if there's no need?
We've traveled the short distance
from need to greed.

NINETEENTH SUNDAY OF THE YEAR
Luke 12:32-48

The Hebrew was told, "Choose life!"
No one told him it would be expensive.
Children, and wisdom, don't come cheaply.
But the world still has parents and students.
They must think it's worth it.

TWENTIETH SUNDAY OF THE YEAR
Luke 12:49-53

Jesus' words are quite emphatic
but also enigmatic!
When all our arguments and bitterness shall
    cease
his final word for us is peace.

TWENTY-FIRST SUNDAY OF THE YEAR
Luke 13:22-30

We are the portly faithful
who can't believe you go to hell
for living it up and eating well!
(P.S. Jesus liked banquets.)

TWENTY-SECOND SUNDAY OF THE YEAR
Luke 14:1, 7-14

He puts the proud to shame
and then invites the crippled and the lame
to share the party. It's plain to see
that the Lord's idea of VIP
is upside down.

TWENTY-THIRD SUNDAY OF THE YEAR
Luke 14:25-33

Make a buck with Jesus.
Praise the Lord without a loss.
Push Christianity
with a featherweight cross.

TWENTY-FOURTH SUNDAY OF THE YEAR
Luke 15:1-32

Jesus, door that opens wide,
gate of pasture green inside,
water washing sins away,
sun that rises on a new day.

TWENTY-FIFTH SUNDAY OF THE YEAR
Luke 16:1-13

To split up God and money
just doesn't seem fair.
Must I really choose, Lord—
saint or millionaire?
In God we trust.
For gold we lust.

171

TWENTY-SIXTH SUNDAY OF THE YEAR
Luke 16:19-31

Is the hottest place in hell
for the rich who didn't care?
No. It's reserved for those who didn't know
the poor were even there.

TWENTY-SEVENTH SUNDAY OF THE YEAR
Luke 17:5-10

There must be some good reason
why God made us, stayed with us, sent his Son.
There is. Faith means, among other things,
that God's work, his purpose, will be done.

TWENTY-EIGHTH SUNDAY OF THE YEAR
Luke 17:11-19

The blind will see;
the bound will be free—
all this if faith is given.
And peace of mind
and hope of heaven.

TWENTY-NINTH SUNDAY OF THE YEAR
Luke 18:1-8

The widow wouldn't give up.
She wearied the unjust judge.
God is easier. No need to fear.
Pour out your heart. The Lord will hear.

THIRTIETH SUNDAY OF THE YEAR
Luke 18:9-14

It's easy to see
the Pharisee lacked humility.
But not a certain generosity!
(Do we pay tithes of all that we possess?)

THIRTY-FIRST SUNDAY OF THE YEAR
Luke 19:1-10

He favored the lowly, all those
who surely weren't among life's winners.
And his enemies said of him,
"This man eats with sinners!"
At his table there's room for you and me.
R.S.V.P.

THIRTY-SECOND SUNDAY OF THE YEAR
Luke 20:27-38

There's another line, too:
It tells of Jesus
"who for us men and our salvation
came down from heaven."
He came for us women, too.

THIRTY-THIRD SUNDAY OF THE YEAR
Luke 21:5-19

The story of creation:
God made the world
for us to enjoy it.
Man made a bomb
which now can destroy it.

CHRIST THE KING
Luke 23:35-43

We are a mixed up lot.
Happy and doomed. Sinners and saints.
But he made us, and incredibly loves us.
No wonder we hope.

Other Solemnities and Feasts of the Lord

ASH WEDNESDAY
Matthew 6:1-6, 16-18

We tend to trumpet
our good deeds,
to let the world know
we've done them.
The gospel suggests
a more modest approach.

PRESENTATION OF THE LORD (February 2)
Luke 2:22-40

A young couple in the Temple
present, without fanfare, their first-born son.
But Simeon knows that with this child
salvation has begun.

ST. JOSEPH (March 19)
Matthew 1:16, 18-21, 24

So many pratfalls, so many pitfalls
in a single walk through life!
How can you avoid them?
You can't. There's even a precipice called
  death.
The answer is faith.

ANNUNCIATION OF THE LORD (March 25)
Luke 1:26-38

The Lord himself will give a sign
that his will prevails, and all will be well.
A virgin shall bring forth a son
and his name shall be Emmanuel.
(And every child born of love
still bears this promise from above.)

BIRTH OF ST. JOHN THE BAPTIST (June 24)

John is a trumpet, John is a shout,
telling us all what God is about—
John is a cutting edge, a sword:
"Hear ye! Hear ye the word of the Lord."

STS. PETER AND PAUL, APOSTLES (June 29)

Peter might wish
to give the job back.
The sheep are not docile
and Paul's on his back.
Persevere. The Lord is still near!

TRANSFIGURATION (August 6)

A vision in the sky
to strengthen those who soon would see him
   die?
A story of the way their grief
turned into absolute belief
that he was risen? Who knows.
With the Bible, that's the way it goes.

ASSUMPTION (August 15)
Luke 11:27-28

And you can call her mother.
Fairest of them all.
Used to children,
she'll answer when you call.

TRIUMPH OF THE CROSS (September 14)
John 3:13-17

There is another approach in the gospel
called the folly of the cross.
It calls for strength through weakness
and counts earthly gains as loss.
(We must try it sometime.)

ALL SAINTS (November 1)
Matthew 5:1-12

"Even saints
turn into sinners
when they miss
their customary dinners."
That's us, Lord, be patient.

ALL SOULS (November 2)

Yes, we believe in heaven
but all the data given
on what happens when we die
is not—well, too helpful.
(In the end, just leave it up to God.)

DEDICATION OF ST. JOHN LATERAN
(November 9)

Take our gifts is what we sing
as bread and wine and tithes we bring.
But the gospel has another line.
It says that giving is just fine—
if the giver is at peace.

IMMACULATE CONCEPTION
(December 8)
Luke 1:26-38

O little town of Nazareth,
we visit thee still,
and ponder where a maiden fair
said yes to the Father's will.

OTHER RESOURCES FOR PREACHING AND TEACHING

Seasonal Illustrations for Preaching and Teaching
Donald L. Deffner

Paper, $11.95
144 pages, 5½" x 8½"
ISBN 0-89390-234-9

"Jesus told stories. Why don't we?" asks the author.
Preachers and teachers: use this book of sermon illustrations to get the attention of your listeners and enrich their understanding of the Sunday readings. Includes "Criteria for the Use of Illustrations."

Sermons for Sermon Haters
Andre Papineau

Paper, $10.95
184 pages, 5½" x 8½"
ISBN 0-89390-229-2

It's a preacher's dream—to turn on the turned off. That's Andre Papineau's specialty. In his new book,
Sermons for Sermon Haters, he shows you how to break open the Gospel in ways that reach even the most jaded.

The Mighty Mustard Bush
Kenneth Guentert

Paper, $8.95
144 pages, 5½" x 8½"
ISBN 0-89390-184-9

Whether you need inspiration for a homily or a new outlook on a season, break out your copy of *The Mighty Mustard Bush* and read just one chapter. The author's biblical sensibility, combined with his down-to-earth wit, will get you going every time.

Order from your local bookseller, or use the order form on the last page.